Harcourt Health and Fitness

Activity Book
Grade 4

Harcourt
SCHOOL PUBLISHERS

Orlando • Austin • New York • San Diego • Toronto • London

Visit *The Learning Site!*
www.harcourtschool.com

Contents

Body Systems at Work

Directions

- Use lesson vocabulary in the Word Bank to complete each **Summary**.
- Read the section directions to complete each **Lesson Details**.

Word Bank

brain	cell	nerves	nutrients	trait
bronchi	diaphragm	nervous system	skeletal system	
capillaries	esophagus	nucleus	spine	

Lesson 1 | pp. 4-9

Summary A characteristic passed on to you from your parents is a _____.

The _____ of each cell contains your inherited plan. The smallest

working part of your body is a _____.

Lesson Details Use pages 6 and 7 in your text to complete the graphic organizer to show how the body is organized.

(cells) ➡ (_____) ➡ (_____) ➡ (_____)

Lesson 2 | pp. 12-14

Summary The body system that coordinates all your activities is the

_____. Thinking, movement, and heart rate are controlled by

the organ known as the _____. _____ are bundles of fibers
that carry messages through the body.

Lesson Details Use the information on page 13 of your text to complete the chart.

Part of Brain	Function
	controls thinking, _____, _____, _____
cerebellum	_____
	controls _____, _____, growth

Lesson 3 | pp. 16-19

Summary During digestion, food is broken down into _____. The

_____ pushes food to the stomach.

Lesson Details Study the pictures and the captions on pages 17 and 18. Explain how
the digestive and circulatory systems work together to get nutrients to cells.

_____

_____

_____

Lesson 4 | pp. 20-23

Summary The two tubes of the trachea are _____. The muscle that helps

you breathe is the _____. _____ are the tiniest blood vessels.

Lesson Details Use page 23 of your text to help you fill in the table.

Type of Blood Cell	Function
	carry oxygen to all parts of the body
white blood cells	

Lesson 5 | pp. 24-26

Summary The body system known as the _____ supports your body.

Your pelvis, leg bones, and _____ work together to let you stand and walk.

Lesson Details Study the diagrams on pages 24 and 25. Draw a line between each
type of muscle and the bone it moves.

Muscles	Bones
abdominal muscles	tibia
deltoid	humerus
elbow flexors	pelvis
knee flexors	radius

Name _____

Sequence

Reflex Action

Your nervous system is always working, even when you are asleep. It picks up information about your environment and sends messages that cause your muscles to respond. It keeps your heartbeat and breathing going.

Sometimes you react to changes in your environment after you think about them. Suppose you are playing softball and you are at bat. The ball comes toward you. Sensory neurons in your eyes send messages to your brain through your spinal cord. Your brain sends the message "Swing!" back through your spinal cord to the motor neurons that cause your arm muscles to move.

Sometimes you react to changes without thinking about them. Your brain is not directly involved. This type of reaction is called a reflex. Reflexes keep us from harming ourselves. Suppose you accidentally touch a hot stove. Sensory neurons in your fingers carry the message of too much heat to sensory neurons in your spinal cord. Then the message passes to relay neurons in your spinal cord. These neurons pass the message to motor neurons in your spinal cord. Motor neurons carry the message out of your spinal cord to muscles in your arm. Your arm bends to move your fingers away from the source of danger.

Fill in the graphic organizer to show how messages travel when you touch a hot stove. Use the names of the two types of neurons. The first box is done for you.

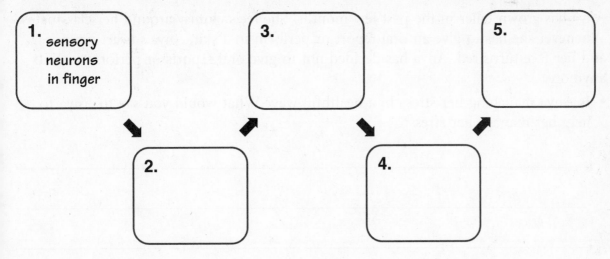

1. sensory neurons in finger

2.

3.

4.

5.

Life Skill
Manage Stress

Steps for Managing Stress

1. Know what stress feels like and what causes it.

2. Try to determine the cause of the stress.

3. Prepare to handle a stressful situation.

4. Think positively rather than negatively.

Use the steps to help these students manage stress.

A. Devon is on a soccer team. Devon has not grown as much as his teammates, who are stronger and able to kick the ball farther. Although Devon is a fast runner, he is worried that he will be dropped from the team. He has trouble sleeping the night before every soccer game.

- Explain how Devon can manage his feelings of stress.

_____

_____

_____

B. Anya has grown taller in the past few months. She feels clumsy around her classmates. Whenever she has to give an oral report or perform in a skit, Anya's heart pounds and her face turns red. Anya has decided not to give oral reports or perform in skits anymore.

- Is Anya managing her stress in a healthful way? What would you say to Anya to help her manage her stress?

_____

_____

_____

_____

Name _____

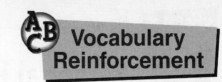

Multiple Choice

A. Circle the letter of the correct answer.

1. Messages are carried through the body by ____.

   A arteries   **C** nerves

   B the brain   **D** veins

2. Air moves first from the nose to the ____.

   F bronchi   **H** diaphragm

   G trachea   **J** esophagus

3. ____ carry blood away from the heart.

   A Capillaries   **C** Muscles

   B Arteries   **D** Veins

4. Food is NOT broken down in the ____.

   F esophagus   **H** small intestine

   G mouth   **J** stomach

5. The ____ protects the brain from injury.

   A muscular system   **C** spine

   B nerves   **D** skull

6. The movement of your ____ moves air in and out of your lungs.

   F esophagus   **H** diaphragm

   G heart   **J** stomach

B. Explain your answer to question 6.

_____

_____

_____

_____

_____

Name _____

Personal Health

Quick Study

Directions

• Use lesson vocabulary in the Word Bank to complete each **Summary**.
• Read the section directions to complete each **Lesson Details**.

Word Bank

consumer	plaque	retina
lens	reliable	epidermis
dermis	advertising	cavities

Lesson 1 pp. 32-35

Summary Caring for your skin is important to your health. This includes protecting

the top layer of skin, called the _____, and the bottom layer, called the

_____.

Lesson Details Use the information on pages 32–33 to complete the table. The first line has been completed for you.

Feature	Description and Function
epidermis	the top layer of skin, which keeps moisture in and germs out
dermis	
sweat gland	
oil gland	
pore	
hair	

Lesson 2 pp. 36-41

Summary Caring for your teeth includes removing sticky _____ from

them to prevent holes called _____ from forming.

Lesson Details On a separate sheet of paper, write a list of habits you can use to keep your teeth and gums healthy. Draw a picture for each habit to help you remember to do the activity.

| Lesson 3 | pp. 42–45

Summary Light enters the eye through the pupil. Once inside, the light passes

through the _____, which bends the light. This focuses an image onto

the back part of the eye, called the _____.

Lesson Details Review page 44. List the sequence of events involved in hearing. Begin with a sound that is produced, and end with the brain interpreting the information.

_____

_____

_____

_____

| Lesson 4 | pp. 48–50

Summary When you buy health products, it is important to be a wise _____.

Research products instead of believing what you see and hear in _____.

Lesson Details Use pages 48–50 to answer the following questions.

What type of product information in an ad might be helpful? _____

_____

What are some tricks that an advertiser may use to get you to buy a product?

_____

_____

| Lesson 5 | pp. 52–54

Summary To get facts about health products or information, use _____ sources, such as doctors, health journals, or government health organizations.

Lesson Details Suppose you want to learn why cavities form in teeth. How would you find reliable health information? What sources would you use? Write your answer on another sheet of paper.

Identify Main Idea and Details

Sunny Solutions

The sun is shining and it's a beautiful summer day. You're ready to grab your swimsuit or basketball and head outside for some fun in the sun. Before you go, don't forget to also grab some sunscreen. One of the most important health decisions you can make is choosing to protect your body's largest organ—your skin.

Wearing sunscreen is an important part of caring for your skin. Sunlight can cause skin damage, including wrinkles and skin cancer. That's where quality sunscreen can help. Sunscreens reduce or block the damaging effects of the sun's rays. The chemicals that make up a sunscreen protect your skin from the sun. A good-quality sunscreen will absorb, scatter, and reflect sunlight before it reaches your skin. A sunscreen with SPF 30 will allow you to stay in the sun 30 times longer without burning than if you didn't wear sunscreen. So before heading outside, be sure to save your skin by taking along the sunscreen.

Use the graphic organizer. Fill in the main idea and supporting details of the passage.

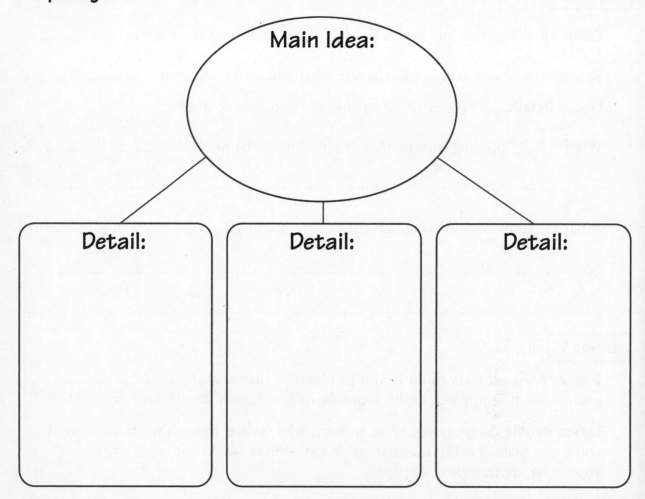

Main Idea:

Detail:

Detail:

Detail:

Problem Solving

Life Skill
Communicate

Steps for Communicating

1. Understand your audience.

2. Give a clear message.

3. Listen carefully and answer any questions.

4. Gather feedback.

Use the steps to tell how these students should communicate their health needs.

A. Marissa was practicing softball with her friends, Latoya and Lina. Marissa was talking with Latoya when Lina threw her the ball. Not knowing the ball was coming, Marissa didn't turn to catch it, and it hit the side of her ear. Marissa felt okay then, but a few hours later her ear started to hurt and make a ringing sound.

• Should Marissa tell anyone about her ear? If so, how should she communicate the information?

_____

_____

_____

_____

B. A month ago, Tony got contact lenses for his birthday. Getting the contacts into his eyes has been tricky, and he still has difficulty with the task. After he gets the contacts in, his eyes are very red from his struggle. He had wanted contacts for two years and is afraid that if he tells his parents about his trouble, he will have to wear his glasses again. When Tony's father asked about his red eyes one morning, Tony said that he was just feeling really tired.

• Will the way Tony communicated help solve his problem? Does it show that he is trustworthy? How should Tony communicate about the problem he is having with his eyes?

_____

_____

_____

_____

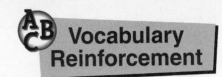

Use Word Meanings

A. Unscramble the underlined word to complete the following sentences.

1. Sally wanted to buy the toothpaste after seeing the danigvister on television.

   _____

2. Matt scraped his outer layer of skin, the reempidis, when he fell on the sidewalk.

   _____

3. The lipup is the opening in the eye that allows light to enter.

   _____

4. Leslie studied the skin's bottom layer, called the misder, for her science fair project.

   _____

5. Rachel is nearsighted because her snel focuses images in front of her retina.

   _____

6. Wayne liked the smooth feeling of his teeth after the dentist removed the sticky qualep from his teeth.

   _____

7. Being a wise runscome means that you research products before you buy them.

   _____

8. Tanya's father told her that eating too much candy would cause her to get vicaties in her teeth.

   _____

9. The nerita is the part of the eye that sends images to the brain through nerve signals.

   _____

B. Choose three of the vocabulary words from Part A. Write a paragraph using the three words.

_____

_____

_____

_____

_____

Name _____

Quick
Study

Food and Your Health

Directions
- Use lesson vocabulary in the Word Bank to complete each **Summary**.
- Read the directions provided to complete each **Lesson Details**.

Word Bank

balanced diet	food guide pyramid	ingredients	portion	vitamins
carbohydrates	food poisoning	minerals	proteins	water
fats	habits	nutritious	serving	

Lesson 1 | pp. 60-64

Summary Your body needs nutrients for growth, energy, and good health. The six

important kinds of nutrients found in food are _____, _____,

_____, _____, _____, and _____.

Lesson Details Under the name of each nutrient, list three foods that are good
sources of that nutrient.

Carbohydrates	Fats	Proteins
1. _____	1. _____	1. _____
2. _____	2. _____	2. _____
3. _____	3. _____	3. _____

Lesson 2 | pp. 66-71

Summary The _____ is a tool you can use to plan

a(n) _____. A(n) _____ is a measured amount of food

recommended for a meal or a snack. A(n) _____ is the amount of
food you might want to eat or the amount you might be served.

Lesson Details Look at pages 68–69.
From which food group should you eat the greatest number of servings each day?

How many servings? _____

Name _____

| **Lesson 3** | pp. 72–75 |

Summary You form healthful eating _____ by making good food choices.

Lesson Details Underline the healthful snack choices among the foods below.

rice cakes   dried fruit   low-fat yogurt   candy bar   nuts and seeds   soda

| **Lesson 4** | pp. 78–83 |

Summary Product labels can be used to determine how _____ a

particular food is. Labels also show the _____, or all the things used to make the food.

Lesson Details Use the information on the cereal label on page 81 to answer the questions.

How much cereal makes up one serving? _____

How much fat is in one serving of cereal? _____

How much protein is in 2 cups of cereal? _____

| **Lesson 5** | pp. 84–86 |

Summary Eating a food that contains germs can cause _____.

Lesson Details Choose two of the tips for handling food safely on page 85. For each, draw a picture to help you remember it. Write the tip under your picture.

_____   _____

Compare and Contrast

Fats and Carbohydrates

Your body needs nutrients for growth, energy, and good health. Fats and carbohydrates are two of the six nutrients that your body gets from foods.

Fats are the nutrient that gives your body the most energy per gram of food. Fats are found in food made from plants and in food made from animals. Fats can be found in oils and butter. Meat, cheese, and whole milk also have fat. Your body uses fat to store extra energy.

Carbohydrates are also used by the body for energy. In fact, they are the nutrient that is the main source of energy for the body. Starches and sugars are both carbohydrates. Carbohydrates are mainly found in food made from plants. Fruits, cereals, breads, and potatoes are good sources of carbohydrates.

Using the graphic organizer, list the ways fats and carbohydrates are alike and the ways they are different.

Compare and Contrast

Alike	Different

Life Skill
Make Responsible Decisions

Steps for Responsible Decision Making

1. Find out about the choices you could make.

2. Eliminate choices that are against your family's rules.

3. Ask yourself: What could happen with each choice? Does the choice show good character?

4. Make what seems to be the best choice.

Use the steps to help students make responsible decisions.

A. Cory walks home from school with his friends. Lately his friends have been stopping at a fast-food restaurant to order French fries each day. Cory's family allows only healthful snacks after school. Cory decides it can't hurt to have French fries every day, so he goes with his friends.

• Did Cory make the best choice? Why or why not?

_____

_____

_____

_____

_____

B. Maria and her cousin have just done several errands at the mall. Maria's mom gave Maria money for a healthful lunch at the mall. Maria sees a hair clip in a mall store that she would really like to have. If she skipped lunch and spent her lunch money on the clip, she could afford it.

• Use the Steps for Making Responsible Decisions to help Maria decide what to do.

_____

_____

_____

_____

_____

Name _____

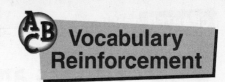
Use Word Meanings

Choose the term that best matches each definition. Write the correct term in the blank to the left of the definition. Use each term once.

balanced diet	food guide pyramid	ingredients	proteins
carbohydrates	food poisoning	minerals	serving
fats	habit	portion	water

_____ 1. Nutrients that are your body's main source of energy

_____ 2. A nutrient necessary for life, it carries away waste.

_____ 3. A measured amount of food recommended for a meal or a snack

_____ 4. A tool used to plan a healthful diet

_____ 5. An illness caused by germs in food

_____ 6. Something you do so often you don't even think about it

_____ 7. Nutrients used to build and repair cells

_____ 8. The things used when you prepare a food

_____ 9. Nutrients that provide the most energy per gram of food

_____ 10. A diet made up of foods from each food group

_____ 11. Calcium and iron are examples of this type of nutrient.

_____ 12. The amount of food you are served for a meal

CHAPTER **4**

Name _____

Fitness and Activity

Quick Study

Directions
- Use lesson vocabulary in the Word Bank to complete each **Summary**.
- Read the section directions to complete each **Lesson Details**.

Word Bank

| posture | rest | Activity Pyramid | anaerobic | aerobic |

Lesson 1 pp. 92-96

Summary You can prevent pain by using good _____ when you stand, when you sit, and when you lift and carry.

Lesson Details Look at the Good Posture Tips on page 93. Rewrite the tips on a sheet of paper. Draw a picture for each tip to help you remember how to use good posture.

_____

_____

_____

_____

Lesson 2 pp. 98-103

Summary _____ exercise causes you to breathe deeply and makes your

heart beat faster. _____ exercise builds muscle strength. These exercises

are short, intense activities. When you get enough _____, your mind and body feel at their best.

Name _____

Lesson Details Use the information on the Three Basic Parts of
Physical Fitness on page 99 to complete the table.

Three Basic Parts of Physical Fitness	Example

Lesson 3 pp. 106-110

Summary The _____ can help you choose activities to include
in your exercise program.

Lesson Details Look at pages 106–107. Explain why a pyramid shape is a better
choice for the Activity Pyramid than a square.

_____

_____

_____

Name _____

Identify Cause and Effect

Kids and Backpacks

Back-to-school should not mean backache and pain. But for kids who use backpacks, it could mean a visit to the doctor. In fact, now that many kids are using backpacks, backpack-related aches and pains are on the rise. An overloaded backpack can strain your back muscles, especially if it is not worn properly.

To wear a backpack properly, you should center it evenly in the middle of your back. Wear both shoulder straps, and make sure they are snug but not too tight. Straps that are too tight can cause the pack to ride up on your neck.

Use the waist belt. Waist belts can distribute the weight of your backpack to your lower body so that your hips and legs bear some of the load. Otherwise, your back may be strained, and you might begin to round your shoulders.

Load your pack with the heaviest items next to your back. This way, the pack won't cause you to lean backward or lose your balance.

Using the graphic organizer, fill in the effects of wearing a backpack incorrectly.

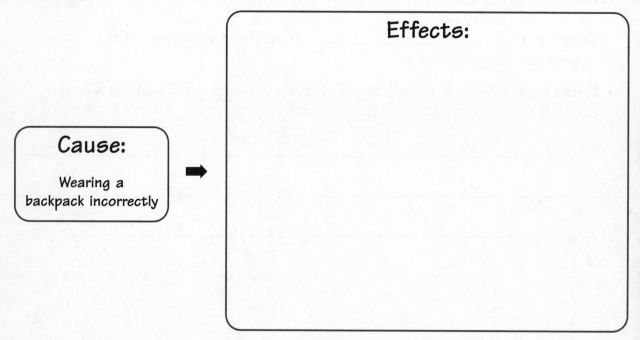

Cause:

Wearing a
backpack incorrectly

Effects:

Name _____

Life Skill

Set Goals

Steps for Setting Goals

1. Choose a goal.

2. List steps to meet the goal. Determine how long it will take to meet the goal.

3. Check your progress as you work toward your goal.

4. Reflect on and evaluate your progress toward the goal.

Use the steps to help these students set fitness goals.

A. Trish wants to become stronger. She is a swimmer, and having strong arms could help her swim faster. She swims every day after school but doesn't do any other physical activity.

• Explain what steps Trish could take to achieve her goal.

_____

_____

_____

_____

_____

B. Larry wants to get in shape, so he decides to begin running five miles every day after school. He has never run before, but he feels that he could do it. Larry begins running, but after 15 minutes, he is gasping and has wobbly legs. Larry is in pain.

• Was Larry's goal responsible? Explain. Tell what a better goal would have been.

_____

_____

_____

_____

_____

Name _____

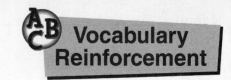

Fitness Find

There are nine terms about fitness hidden forward, backward, across, down, and diagonally in the puzzle. Circle each term, and then write it in the correct sentence below.

A	H	T	G	N	E	R	T	S	E	L	C	S	U	M
E	N	D	U	R	A	N	C	E	H	Y	T	A	X	H
R	W	A	N	F	L	E	X	I	B	I	L	I	T	Y
O	R	A	N	A	E	R	O	B	I	C	F	I	T	N
B	C	I	R	B	O	R	E	A	N	D	R	R	T	W
I	G	H	S	M	U	Z	B	A	R	J	A	E	X	K
C	S	T	E	R	U	T	S	O	P	K	E	S	B	Z
D	I	M	A	R	Y	P	Y	T	I	V	I	T	C	A

1. Before exercising, it is important to _____ for five to ten minutes.

2. Running and swimming are examples of _____ exercise.

3. Working muscles harder for longer periods without getting tired is

   _____.

4. Push-ups and pull-ups help build _____.

5. The _____ lists activities that can help you plan a fitness program.

6. Sleep and _____ help the body and mind relax.

7. _____ exercises are short, intense activities.

8. Good _____ is holding your body in a balanced way when you stand, sit, and move.

9. Stretching is a good exercise to help increase _____.

Safe at Home

Directions
- Use lesson vocabulary in the Word Bank to complete each **Summary**.
- Read the section directions to complete each **Lesson Details**.

Word Bank

emergency	hazard	lifeguard	family emergency plan

Lesson 1 | pp. 116-120

Summary If an _____ happens, tell an adult or call 911. Deciding on escape routes from your home should be part of your

_____.

Lesson Details The parts of a family emergency plan are listed in the left column. The reason each part is important is listed in the right column. Draw a line to match each part with the reason it is important.

Know your family contact   to know how to prepare for disasters.

Know what could happen   so family members will know everyone is safe.

Learn how to turn off utilities   to let someone in another city know you are safe.

Decide on escape routes   to get out of your home quickly.

Choose two meeting places   to prevent danger from water, gas, and electricity.

Lesson 2 | pp. 122-125

Summary A slippery floor is an example of a _____ that can lead to a fall.

Lesson Details Hazardous Hilda does not know her safety rules. Listed below are five unsafe actions. Help Hilda keep herself and others safe. Write the safety rule for each behavior. The first one is done for you.

1. Hilda wants to stick a fork in the toaster to get out a piece of stuck bread. Don't stick metal objects into electrical appliances.

2. Hilda has a cough, so she reaches for the cough syrup.

_____

3. Hilda leaves her backpack in the doorway.

_____

4. With bare hands, Hilda reaches for a hot cup in the microwave.

_____

5. Hilda decides to spray a big bug with insect spray when her parents aren't around.

_____

| **Lesson 3** | pp. 128–130 |

Summary At a swimming pool, the _____ has the authority to tell people to follow the rules.

Lesson Details Use pp. 128–130 to complete the graphic organizer.

Main Idea:
Practicing water safety can help prevent injury.

Details:

1. Obey the _____.

2. Don't jump into the pool _____.

3. Dive only into water _____ feet deep or more.

4. Don't dive from the _____ of a pool.

5. Wear a _____ when you are on a boat.

Name _____

Sequence

How Accidents Happen

Have you ever lined up dominoes and then touched one and watched all of them fall? What happens if you remove one domino from the line or move it so that the domino before it cannot touch it? All the other dominoes that follow will remain standing.

In the same way, many injuries occur because of an order, or sequence, of events. One event leads to another event. Here is a sequence.

1. the situation: the first thing that leads to the accident

2. the risky habit: a habit that is unsafe

3. the risky act: a behavior that is unsafe

4. the accident: the result of the risky act

5. the injury: the result of the accident

The following sentences that describe an accident are not in the correct order. Copy the graphic organizer below, and use it to put the events in the correct sequence. Then write one way each of the first three events could be changed to prevent the injury.

Ben leaves the floor wet. Ben's sister breaks her wrist when she falls. Ben lets his dog in from the rain, and the dog drips water on the floor. Ben's sister slips and falls on the wet floor. Ben doesn't notice the water on the floor, because he often doesn't notice unsafe conditions.

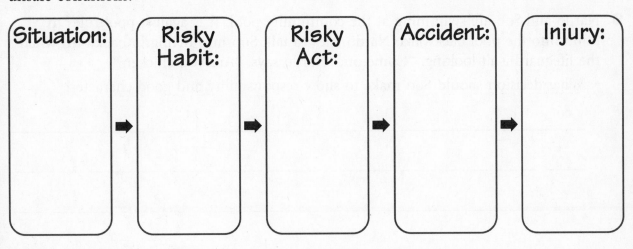

Situation: _____

Risky Habit: _____

Risky Act: _____

Name _____

Life Skill

Make Responsible Decisions

Steps for Making Responsible Decisions

1. Find out about the choices you could make.

2. Eliminate choices that are against your family rules.

3. Ask yourself: What is the possible result of each choice? Does the choice show good character?

4. Make what seems to be the best choice.

Use the steps to help these students make responsible decisions.

A. Zalika has friends over for a slumber party. Some of the girls want to place lighted candles around Zalika's bedroom. This is against Zalika's family rules. Zalika's parents are already asleep. "Your parents won't know," says one of the girls.

• Explain what would be the most responsible decision for Zalika to make.

_____

_____

_____

_____

_____

B. Nardo and Soo are swimming at the community pool. It is against pool rules to jump into the pool backward. Nardo tries to talk Soo into diving in backward when the lifeguard isn't looking. "Come on," Nardo says. "Are you chicken?"

• What decision should Soo make to show responsibility and good character?

_____

_____

_____

_____

_____

Name _____

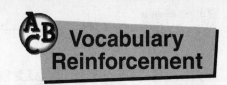

Matching

Column A is a list of words and phrases you have studied in Chapter 5. Column B is a list of statements that describe the words and phrases in Column A. In the blank beside each word or phrase in Column A, write the letter of the statement that describes it.

Column A	Column B
_____ emergency	**a.** Follow this if you need to get out of your home quickly.
_____ emergency supply kit	**b.** Use these steps if someone is drowning.
_____ family emergency plan	**c.** Part of this is knowing your community's warning signals.
_____ hazard	**d.** You obey this person when you swim.
_____ lifeguard	**e.** An example of this is wearing a life jacket when on a boat.
_____ poisons	**f.** Keep a flashlight, food, and water in this.
_____ reach and throw	**g.** If this happens, tell an adult or call 911.
_____ safety measure	**h.** Do this if your clothes catch fire.
_____ stop, drop, and roll	**i.** Keep these out of the reach of young children.
_____ escape route	**j.** An example of this is an overloaded electrical outlet.

Safe Away from Home

Quick Study

Directions
• Use lesson vocabulary in the Word Bank to complete each **Summary**.
• Read the directions provided to complete each **Lesson Details**.

Word Bank

air bag	flood	hurricane	tornado
bully	gang	lightning	weapon

Lesson 1 pp. 136-140

Summary During a _____, the force of the water can knock you off

your feet. Go to a basement or a closet if there is a _____. To avoid

getting hit by _____, go indoors during a thunderstorm. You can

prepare for a _____ by moving inland.

Lesson Details For each situation, write what you should do to stay safe.

Situation	What You Should Do
You see a baby raccoon while camping.	
You are hiking where there are ticks.	
You are deciding what to wear on a very hot day.	
You hear thunder while playing outside.	

Lesson 2 pp. 142-145

Summary Children are safer in the back seat of a motor vehicle because the

_____ can injure them during a collision.

Lesson Details Cross out the wrong word in each sentence. Write the correct word or phrase in the blank.

1. When you ride in a motor vehicle, fasten the safety belt across

   your stomach. _____

2. Pass on the right when you ride your bike. _____

3. When you skate, cross a street only at a walk. _____

4. Cross the street in back of the school bus. _____

5. Ride in the front seat of a motor vehicle. _____

6. Wear dark-colored clothing when you ride your bike. _____

| Lesson 3 | pp. 148–152

Summary A _____ teases people in a mean way. A member of a

_____ might use drugs and carry a _____.

Lesson Details Use the list on page 149 to complete the graphic organizer. For each action by a bully, choose the two ways that you think would work best for dealing with the bully. Write the ways below the action. One is done for you.

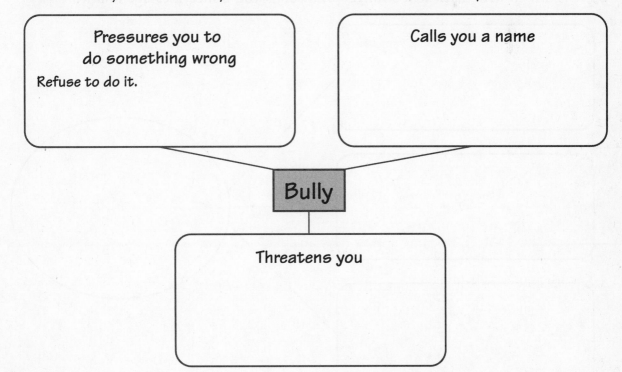

Name _____

Draw Conclusions

Safety Online

Suppose you receive an e-mail from someone you don't know. The person says she is 10 years old and wants to be your pen pal. Can you believe what this person is telling you? You can't see or hear the person. What people tell you online may or may not be true.

Some adults who are looking for children to harm use the computer to contact children. They may write nice messages and offer gifts to gain your trust. Then they might send pictures that make you uncomfortable. They may ask to meet you in person.

Follow safety rules when you use the computer. Visit only websites that your parents say are OK. If a person you don't know writes to you, tell your parents. They can tell you if it's safe to write back. Tell your parents if anyone sends you a mean message or one that makes you feel uncomfortable. Never give your last name, address, or phone number on any website (even on those you are allowed to visit) unless your parents have approved.

Which of the following conclusions can you draw from this passage? Write the conclusion in the circle of the graphic organizer. Then write three details.

A. All strangers who write to you online tell lies about themselves.

B. You can stay safe online by following safety rules.

C. It is OK to write back to a stranger who sends you a nice message online.

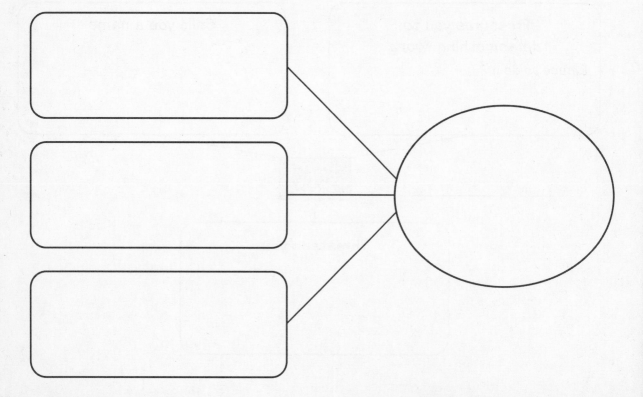

Name _____

Life Skill

Resolve Conflicts

Steps for Resolving Conflicts

1. Use "I" messages to tell how you feel.

2. Listen to the other person. Consider the other person's point of view.

3. Negotiate.

4. Compromise on a solution.

Tell how these students could resolve their conflicts.

A. Jamila and Carlita are working together on a social studies project. Jamila wants to do a skit for their presentation. Carlita wants to make a diorama. The girls start to argue.

- Explain how Jamila and Carlita can come up with a solution that is agreeable to both of them.

_____

_____

_____

_____

_____

B. Austin goes to Nathan's house after school. They are deciding what to do. Nathan wants to play a board game. Austin wants to play basketball. Austin says angrily, "You never want to do what I want!" He looks as if he wants to fight.

- How is Austin not following the Steps for Resolving Conflicts? What can Nathan say to prevent the boys from fighting?

_____

_____

_____

_____

_____

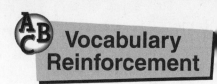

Complete the Puzzle

Use the clues to complete the puzzle.

Across

4. a powerful windstorm

5. a storm that forms over an ocean and covers a large area

7. a person who hurts or frightens others

8. a group of people who often use violence

Down

1. an object that is used to injure or threaten someone

2. an overflow of water onto normally dry land

3. a large release of electricity

6.–7. a safety item that inflates in a motor vehicle during a collision

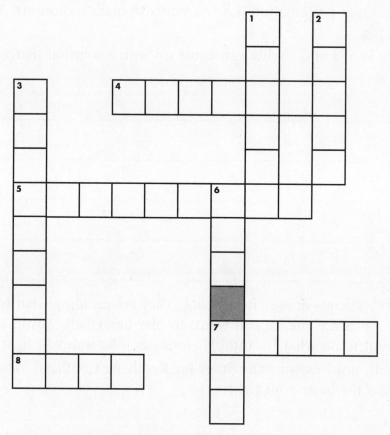

Name _____

Guarding Against Disease

Directions
- Use the vocabulary in the Word Bank to complete each **Summary**.
- Use the directions provided to complete each **Lesson Details**.

Word Bank

disease	pathogens	fungi	antibodies	cancer
bacteria	asthma	infection	viruses	allergy
noncommunicable disease	diabetes	communicable disease	vaccine	immune system
immunity	arthritis	resistance	abstinence	

Lesson 1   pp. 158–160

Summary A condition that damages or weakens part of the body is a

_____. A(n) _____ is a

disease that can spread from person to person. A disease that doesn't spread from

person to person is called a(n) _____.

Lesson Details Complete the table of diseases by writing the following terms:
asthma, chicken pox, pinkeye, diabetes, sickle cell anemia, strep throat.

Noncommunicable	Communicable

Lesson 2   pp. 162–165

Summary _____ cause communicable diseases. _____,

which cause strep throat, and _____, which cause most colds, are two

kinds of pathogens. _____ are the pathogens that cause athlete's foot.

The growth of pathogens somewhere in the body is called a(n) _____.

Lesson Details On a separate sheet of paper, write two sentences. Each sentence should describe one way that pathogens can spread.

Lesson 3 pp. 166–171

Summary The _____ fights disease. _____ are chemicals that the body makes to fight disease. The body's ability to defend itself from disease

is called _____. A(n) _____ can help prevent a disease.

Lesson Details On another sheet of paper, list three healthful habits that help prevent the spread of disease.

Lesson 4 pp. 174–179

Summary Body cells that aren't normal and grow out of control are a part of a

disease called _____. Some people have a(n) _____ to

animals, plants, or foods. _____ is a disease that causes breathing problems. Insulin is not used properly or is not made by your body if you have

_____. _____ is a disease that causes joint pain.

Lesson Details Complete the table by writing the following words: *diabetes, allergies, asthma, arthritis.*

Disease	cancer				
Symptoms	lumps called tumors	stuffy nose, itchy eyes	weakness, tiredness	joint pain	difficulty breathing

Lesson 5 pp. 180–182

Summary Your body has _____, or natural ability to fight diseases.

Avoiding a behavior that can harm your health is called _____.

Lesson Details List two ways to help your body stay well. _____

_____

Name _____

Compare and Contrast

Communicable and Noncommunicable Diseases

Everyone becomes ill once in a while. All diseases damage or weaken a part of the body. Diseases such as colds, the flu, and strep throat can make you sick for days or weeks.

Although everyone becomes ill from disease, not all diseases are the same. Some diseases called communicable diseases spread from person to person. Pinkeye, strep throat, colds, and chicken pox are communicable diseases.

Noncommunicable diseases can't be spread from person to person. Some noncommunicable diseases are caused by pollution. Others are caused by unhealthful habits. Still others are common in families.

Fill in the graphic organizer. Tell how communicable and noncommunicable diseases are alike and how they are different.

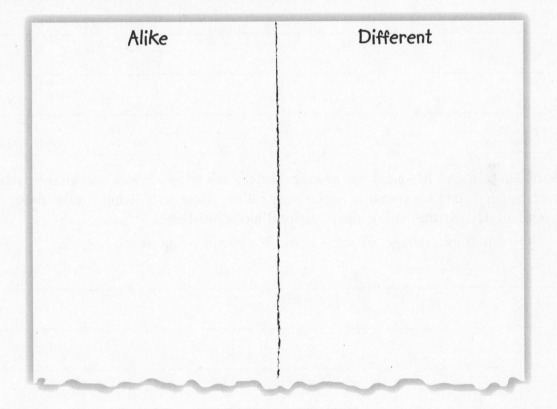

Alike	Different

Name _____

Life Skill
Manage Stress

Steps for Managing Stress

1. Know what stress feels like and what causes it.

2. Try to determine the cause of the stress.

3. Visualize yourself in a more pleasant situation.

4. Think positively rather than negatively.

Use the steps above to help these students manage stress.

A. Jacob fell off his bike. Although he was wearing his helmet, he still got some scrapes and bruises. His doctor will give him stitches to close one large cut. Jacob is feeling a lot of stress about getting stitches.

• How can Jacob deal with his stress?

_____

_____

_____

_____

_____

B. Sunil's best friend has a *chronic* disease. Usually his friend is well and attends school with Sunil. Today his friend is in the hospital for some tests. Sunil thinks about his friend all day. By the end of the day, Sunil has a headache.

• How can Sunil manage his stress about his friend being in the hospital?

_____

_____

_____

_____

_____

Name _____

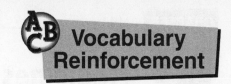

Choose the Correct Word

There are two answer choices for each blank. Choose the one that makes the sentence true, and write it in the blank.

1. Colds and the flu are both [communicable diseases/noncommunicable diseases]

    _____.

2. Avoiding an unhealthful behavior is called [resistance/abstinence]

    _____.

3. Athlete's foot is a disease caused by [bacteria/fungi] _____.

4. Chemicals your body makes to fight disease, called [abstinence/antibodies]

    _____, attach themselves to pathogens that enter your body.

5. If you have [asthma/diabetes] _____, your body can't use or make insulin properly.

6. A disease that causes joint pain is [allergies/arthritis] _____.

7. Bacteria are a type of [pathogen/virus] _____.

8. The growth of pathogens somewhere in your body is [immunity/infection]

    _____.

9. _____ [Asthma/Abstinence] is a disease that makes it difficult to breathe.

10. A [disease/resistance] _____ is something that causes the body not to work as it should.

11. A kind of [bacteria/virus] _____ causes strep throat.

12. The body's ability to defend itself against certain pathogens is called

    [immunity/disease] _____.

CHAPTER 8

Name _____

Quick Study

Medicines, Drugs, and Your Health

Directions
- Use lesson vocabulary in the Word Bank to complete each **Summary**.
- Read the directions provided to complete each **Lesson Details**.

Word Bank

addiction	dose	expiration date	marijuana	prescription
caffeine	drug	illegal drug	peer pressure	recovery
cocaine	drug dependence	inhalants	over-the-counter medicines	self-respect

Lesson 1   pp. 188-193

Summary A _____ changes the way the body works.

_____, which you can buy at the store, and

_____ medicines, which a doctor orders, should be taken

with care. Make sure you take the right amount, or _____,

and that the _____ has not passed.

Lesson Details How are drugs and medicines alike? How are they different?

_____

_____

Lesson 2   pp. 194-197

Summary A repeated strong desire for a drug is a sign of _____.

_____ is a drug found in coffee. Fumes from household products used

as drugs are _____.

Lesson Details Write how each of the following drugs affects the body.

Inhalants: _____

_____

Caffeine: _____

_____

| Lesson 3 | pp. 200–204

Summary One drug that is against the law is _____, which comes from

the hemp plant. Another _____ is _____, which comes from

the coca plant. People who need drugs to feel normal have _____.

Lesson Details Below are some effects of drugs. Write *C* if the effect is from cocaine, *M* if from marijuana, and *M* and *C* if from both drugs.

1. _____ affects learning and memory   **3.** _____ causes confusion

2. _____ can cause heart attacks   **4.** _____ can cause cancer

| Lesson 4 | pp. 206–209

Summary People who like themselves have _____. They do not

give in to _____, or do things because their friends want them to.

Lesson Details Write three ways to say *no* to drugs.

I can say, _____

_____

| Lesson 5 | pp. 210–212

Summary People who take drugs can get help. There are many organizations that

can help with _____, or stopping drug use.

Lesson Details Imagine that you have a friend who is using drugs. What should you do? On another sheet of paper, write at least two ways you could help.

Summarize

Medicines

When you get sick, one of the ways you can get better is by taking medicine. There are two main kinds of medicines. The first is the kind your parent or other adult family member might buy for you, called over-the-counter (OTC) medicine. The other is the kind your doctor writes an order for, called prescription medicine.

Over-the-counter medicines are drugs such as pain relievers and cough medicines. If you have a cut, an adult might put OTC antibiotic cream on your cut to keep it from getting infected. You can buy OTC medicines in places like drugstores and grocery stores.

If you have visited the doctor with a health problem, he or she may have prescribed a medicine for you. That means that the doctor wrote an order for a medicine that would help you feel better. Your parent or another adult probably took the prescription to a pharmacy. The pharmacist got the medicine ready.

No matter what kind of medicine you use, you need to be careful with it. Medicine can only help make you better if you take it the way the doctor ordered or the way the label on the OTC medicine tells you to take it. If you take the medicine incorrectly, you might get sick or not get well. For medicine to do its work, the people taking medicine have to do theirs, too.

Add the details and summary to the graphic organizer.

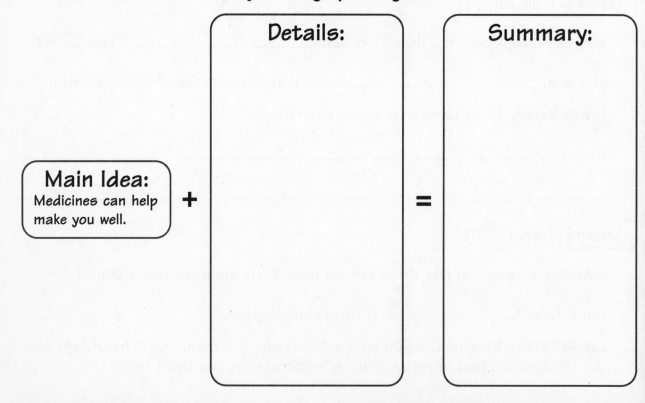

Details:

Summary:

Main Idea:
Medicines can help make you well.

+

=

Life Skill

Refuse

Steps for Refusing OTC Medicines

1. Say *no* firmly, and state your reasons for saying *no*.

2. Remember a consequence, and keep saying *no*.

3. Suggest something else to do.

4. Repeat *no* and walk away.

Tell how these students can use the steps for refusing OTC medicines.

A. Jason tells Ben he has something to show him. He shows Ben some medicine in a bottle. "I got it from Seth," Jason says. "He says it's for coughs but it makes you feel really good."

• What should Ben tell Jason? Write how Ben could use the steps above to help him refuse the medicine.

_____

_____

_____

_____

B. Jennifer is with Marcy when Marcy opens her purse and pulls out a package of pills. "I saw these at home. The package says they give you energy. I really need some energy. Do you want one, too?"

• How could Jennifer say *no*? Write how she could use the steps above to refuse the pills.

_____

_____

_____

_____

_____

_____

Name _____

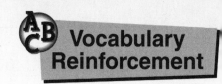

Use Word Meanings

Underline the term that makes the sentence correct.

1. (Recovery Self-respect) is the process of stopping drug use.

2. If you have an (addiction, illegal drug,) you have a craving that makes you use a drug.

3. The drug (cocaine marijuana) is from the hemp plant.

4. A (recovery drug) is a substance that changes the way your body works.

5. Fumes from household products that are used as drugs are (prescription drugs. inhalants.)

6. Two examples of (drug dependence illegal drugs) are cocaine and marijuana.

7. (Over-the-counter medicines Prescription medicines) are drugs you can buy without a doctor's order.

8. When your friends try to get you to do something, that is called (self-respect. peer pressure.)

9. You have (self-respect drug dependence) when you need to take a drug to feel normal.

10. (Caffeine Marijuana) is a drug found in coffee.

Name _____

Quick Study

Harmful Effects of Tobacco and Alcohol

Directions
- Use lesson vocabulary in the Word Bank to complete each **Summary**.
- Read the directions provided to complete each **Lesson Details**.

Word Bank

addiction	alcoholics	messages	responsible
advertisement	alcoholism	nicotine	tar
alcohol	intoxicated	peer pressure	

Lesson 1 pp. 218-223

Summary Tobacco has many harmful chemicals. _____ is a chemical

that speeds up the nervous system. _____ is dark and sticky. It coats the
lungs, making it hard to breathe.

Lesson Details Fill in the chart below with the health problems caused by using
tobacco.

Lesson 2 pp. 224-229

Summary Beer, wine, and liquor all contain a drug called _____. People

who drink too much and become _____ have trouble thinking clearly.

People who are addicted to alcohol have a disease called _____.

Lesson Details List one or more ways heavy drinking can affect each of these body
systems.

Nervous system: _____

Cardiovascular system: _____

Digestive system: _____

| Lesson 3 | pp. 230-233 |

Summary When friends try to get you to do something, you feel _____.

When a friend asks you to smoke, the _____ behavior is to say *no*.

Lesson Details Write two ways you can avoid the pressure to drink alcohol.

1. _____

2. _____

| Lesson 4 | pp. 236-238 |

Summary People who have an _____ to alcohol feel that they must have

it. These people are _____. They need help to stop drinking.

Lesson Details Write two organizations that help people with each of the following addictions.

Tobacco addiction	
Alcohol addiction	

| Lesson 5 | pp. 240-242 |

Summary An _____ can send false _____ that
people who use alcohol and tobacco have more fun.

Lesson Details Write the facts for each of the following ads.

What the Ad Shows	Facts
happy, popular young people enjoying smoking	
friends enjoying sports as they drink a beer	

Name _____

Identify Cause and Effect

Long-Term Use of Tobacco

Whenever tobacco is used, the poison nicotine enters the blood. This drug is addictive—it makes a person crave more nicotine. Nicotine raises the blood pressure, which can lead to heart disease. Tobacco smoke also contains other poisons, such as carbon monoxide, a deadly gas. Carbon monoxide keeps oxygen from reaching the blood. People smoke tobacco in cigarettes, cigars, and pipes.

When a person smokes or breathes other people's smoke, his or her lungs become coated with tar. Over time, the tar can build up enough to block the flow of air to the lungs. This can lead to many lung diseases, such as lung cancer. It can cause the airways in the lungs to become permanently blocked.

Smokeless tobacco is chewing tobacco or snuff. With this form of tobacco, nicotine enters the bloodstream through the blood vessels in the mouth. It can cause sores to form inside the mouth. Over time, these sores can become cancer of the lips, tongue, cheeks, or throat. Smokeless tobacco is even more addictive than smoking tobacco because more nicotine enters the body with each use.

Fill in the graphic organizer with the effects of long-term use of smoking tobacco and smokeless tobacco.

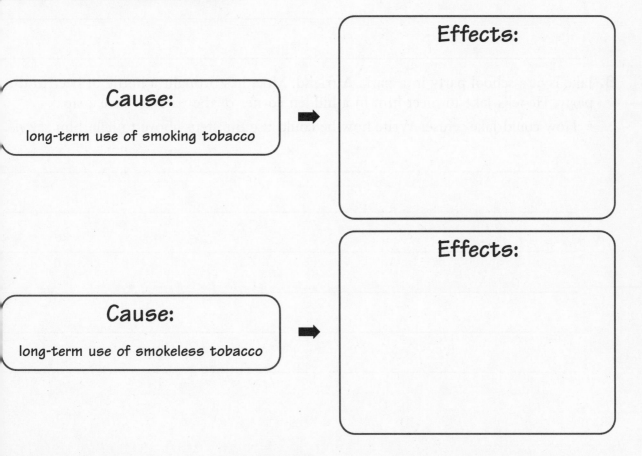

Name _____

Life Skill
Refuse

Steps for Refusing to Use Alcohol and Tobacco

1. Say *no* and tell why not.

2. Suggest something else to do.

3. Reverse the peer pressure.

4. Repeat *no* and walk away. Leave the door open for the other person to join you.

Use the steps to tell how these students could say *no*.

A. Keisha's friend Leilani has a friend named Mel who smokes. One day Keisha and Leilani stop to talk to Mel. Mel pulls out a cigarette and asks Keisha if she wants to try it.

• How could Keisha say *no*? Write the steps that could help her.

_____

_____

_____

_____

_____

B. Jake is at a school party in a park. A friend, Moe, has brought a bottle of beer to the party. He tells Jake to meet him in a hidden corner of the park to have a sip.

• How could Jake refuse? Write how he could use the steps above to help him say *no*.

_____

_____

_____

_____

_____

_____

Name _____

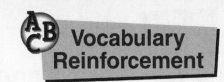

Mapping Terms

A. Use the terms below to fill in the map.

nicotine	alcoholism	messages	tar
responsible	intoxicated	alcohol	alcoholic
advertisements	peer pressure	addiction	

1. _____

may use false _____ to sell these products.

2. Drinking beer, wine, and liquor,

which contain _____, may make a

person _____. The name for the disease people have who cannot stop drinking is

_____. A person with this disease

is a(n) _____.

3. Tobacco contains dangerous chemicals,

such as _____ and

_____.

4. Make _____

decisions. Avoid _____ that

encourages _____ to smoking and drinking.

B. Write a slogan about the dangers of drinking or smoking, using at least two of the vocabulary terms listed above.

Name _____

Your Needs and Feelings

Directions

- Use the vocabulary in the Word Bank to complete each **Summary**.
- Use the section directions to complete each **Lesson Details**.

Word Bank

basic needs	conflict	negotiate	role model	self-control
compassion	conflict resolution	peer pressure	self-concept	
compromise	goal	privacy	self-confidence	

Lesson 1   pp. 248–251

Summary The way you picture yourself is your _____. When you are

sure of yourself, you have _____.

Lesson Details Fill in the ending of each sentence.

A social trait I have is _____.

A mental or emotional trait I have is _____.

A physical trait I have is _____.

Lesson 2   pp. 252–255

Summary The needs that all people have are _____. A social need

you might have is time by yourself, or _____. A _____ is
something you are willing to work for.

Lesson Details There are four basic needs. Fill in the diagram with these needs, and
give an example of each.

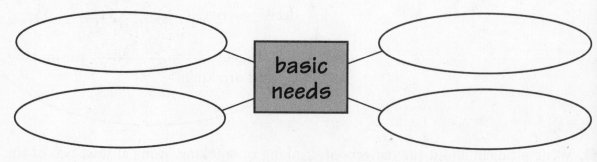

Lesson 3 pp. 256-259

Summary People who express their feelings calmly have _____.

Lesson Details Write the steps to help manage anger.

1. _____   3. _____

2. _____   4. _____

Lesson 4 pp. 260-265

Summary When friends disagree, they have a _____. They can solve

their disagreement through _____. They can work together, or

_____, to find a _____.

Lesson Details How can you find a friend? Write a sentence that tells how.

_____

_____

Lesson 5 pp. 268-272

Summary When you understand the feelings of others, you have

_____. A _____ is someone who

sets a good example.

Lesson Details Write a sentence telling how you can make a difference in your

community or your school. _____

_____

Lesson 6 pp. 274-276

Summary Positive _____ from your friends can help you choose
activities that help yourself and the community.

Lesson Details Write an example of one positive and one negative influence you
could have on a friend.

Positive: _____   Negative: _____

Name _____

Identify Main Idea and Details

Making a Difference

Sometimes, young people don't think they can make a difference in the world. They can, though. They can make a difference in their homes. They can make a difference in their schools. They can make a difference in the community in which they live.

How can you make a difference at home? There are many ways you can make life better for everyone. For instance, how often have you come home and thrown your backpack on the floor or left your room a mess? It doesn't take long to put away your backpack or make your room tidy. Those simple actions can make a big difference at home. If you really want to make a big difference, be a secret helper. Hang up your sister's coat. Clean up a mess your brother made. You might be surprised at how good you feel—and how much people appreciate what you do.

You can make a difference at school, too. Look for chances to help. Most people walk right by other students who are sitting alone. Sometimes they don't even notice a student who is left out. You can change that and make a difference in someone's life. Invite someone who is eating lunch alone to eat with you. At recess, go up to someone who is new at your school. Ask him or her to join you. You'll never know how much difference your kindness might make in someone's life.

You might feel that your community is too large for you to make any difference. You might be surprised at the difference you can make. Little things count. You can put your trash in trash containers. You can help an older neighbor rake leaves or take him or her a plate of cookies you just made. Your moment of kindness can make someone else feel less alone in the world.

Complete the graphic organizer with the main idea and details.

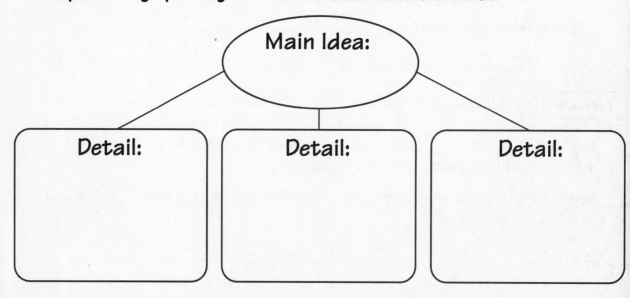

Name _____

Life Skill
Resolve Conflicts

Steps for Resolving Conflicts at School

1. Use "I" messages to tell how you feel.

2. Listen to each other. Consider the other person's point of view.

3. Ask for a mediator.

4. Find a way for both sides to win.

Use the steps to help these students resolve their conflicts.

A. Both Ellen and Rosa want to share a locker with Lana. Each girl says that Lana agreed to share a locker with her. Ellen says, "Lana and I have been friends longer, so we should share a locker." Rosa says, "Lana and I have already talked about how we will decorate our locker."

- Think about how the friends could resolve their conflict. Write the steps that could help them.

_____

_____

_____

_____

_____

B. Carl and Neil are assigned to work together on a report. Carl wants to write a report about World War II. Neil wants to write a report about the space flights to the moon. Neither wants to write about the other person's topic.

- How can Carl and Neil work together? Write how they can use the steps to help them resolve their conflict.

_____

_____

_____

_____

_____

Chapter 10 • Your Needs and Feelings

Name _____

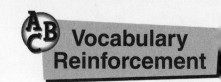

Use Word Meanings

A. Choose the term that makes each sentence correct.

basic needs	goal	conflict	role model
compassion	negotiate	privacy	self-control
compromise	peer pressure	self-confidence	self-concept
conflict resolution			

1. Your _____ is how you picture yourself.

2. You can use _____ to calmly tell how you feel.

3. A positive _____ is a person who sets a good example for others.

4. Positive _____ is helping your friends do something helpful or fun.

5. When people have different needs or wishes, they may have a _____.

6. You have _____ when you understand the feelings of others.

7. A solution in which both sides give up some of what they want is a _____.

8. You _____ when you work together to find a solution to a problem.

9. The four kinds of _____ are social, physical, mental, and emotional.

10. You want _____ when you want to be by yourself.

11. When you and your friends solve a problem between yourselves, you have used

_____.

12. You have a _____ when you are willing to work toward something.

13. _____ is feeling sure of yourself.

B. Write a sentence in which you tell how you can solve any problems between yourself and your friends. Use at least two vocabulary words in your sentence.

_____

Families Together

Name _____

Directions
Use the chapter vocabulary and other terms in the Word Bank to complete each **Summary**.
Read the section directions to complete each **Lesson Details**.

Word Bank

traditions	blended family	peer pressure
nuclear family	extended family	values
single-parent family	communicate	cooperate

Lesson 1 | pp. 282–286

Summary Families can be very different from one another. A family that is made up

of two parents and one or more children is called a _____. A child

or children and only one parent is called a _____. An

_____ consists of parents, children, and other close relatives, such as

grandparents and aunts and uncles. A _____ consists of two single
parents who marry and their children. The various customs that families follow,

such as celebrating events and holidays, are called _____.

Lesson Details Read the paragraph below, and then write a sentence summarizing
the main idea.

　　The role of parents is to take care of the children and to support them.
Children's roles change over time. As they grow older, they are expected to take on
more chores, such as taking out the trash, washing dishes, and doing housework.
They may also be responsible for helping care for younger siblings.

Summary: _____

_____

Lesson 2 pp. 288–291

Summary I can talk to my parents about many things. When my friends push me to do things that I don't want to do, I talk to my parents about how to resist

_____. I feel closer to my parents when I _____ with them.

Lesson Details Fill in the web below with different ways you can communicate with your family.

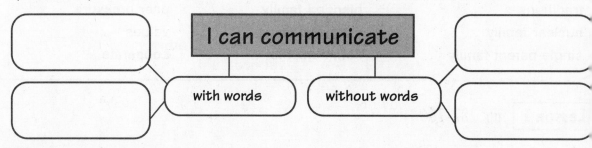

Lesson 3 pp. 294–298

Summary My parents say that honesty is one of the most important _____ that a person can have. To get along well with people, my parents say that I should

learn to _____ with others.

Lesson Details Write one way you can cooperate with each person.

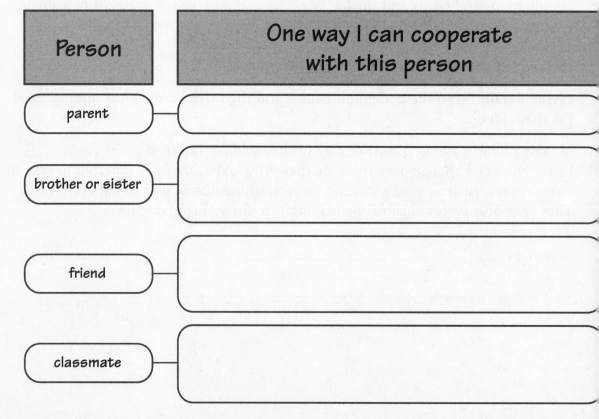

Person	One way I can cooperate with this person
parent	
brother or sister	
friend	
classmate	

ame _____

Focus Skill **Reading Skill**

ummarize

amilies and Health

Your family can help you stay healthy in many ways. Parents or grandparents may ell you to brush your teeth every morning when you get up and every night before ou go to bed. They may remind you to bathe or take a shower every day. When you o these things every day, you develop healthful habits. You will likely keep these habits our whole life.

The adults in your family may help keep you healthy in other ways. You may have certain bedtime. Children often grumble about bedtimes. But going to bed on time elps keep you healthy. You may not know it, but getting enough sleep is very impor-nt for your health. Your body does not feel right—and it does not work right—when ou're tired.

Parents and grandparents may help keep you healthy by having only healthful foods the house. Junk foods usually have lots of fat and sugar. Fat and sugar are not good or your health. They tend to make you gain weight. Adults who care about their hildren's health keep healthful snacks in the house. They may stock up on fruits and egetables—like carrots and celery—for you to snack on. The meals they cook for you on't have a lot of fat. When you get used to eating healthful foods as a child, you're kely to maintain a healthful diet when you grow up.

Getting along with family members also helps keep you healthy. When people get ong, they're happier. They don't have stress. They can deal calmly with problems. amily members who get along help each other. Family members are healthier when ney are calm and work well together.

Write two or three sentences that summarize the main points of this passage.

_____

_____

_____

_____

_____

Chapter 11 • Families Together

Activity Book • 53

Life Skill
Communicate

Steps for Communicating

1. Understand your audience.

2. Give a clear message.

3. Listen carefully, and answer any questions.

4. Gather feedback.

Use the steps to help these students communicate with their families.

A. At 7:00 each evening, Jamie likes to watch his favorite TV program. His brother, who is one year older than Jamie, has just discovered a program on another channel that he wants to watch at 7:00. Lately, Jamie and his brother have been arguing over who gets to watch TV at 7:00.

• What should Jamie do to solve this problem?

_____

_____

_____

B. Linda shares a room with her older sister, Maggie. Linda likes to keep her things in good order. Maggie's things are usually lying around all over the room. When Mom comes into the room, she gets angry about the mess. If Linda is there, Mom takes her anger out on Linda, telling her to clean up the room. Linda tries to tell Mom that the mess is not hers, that it's Maggie's. But her mother is often too angry to listen. "Just clean up this mess," her mother says, and walks out of the room. Linda thinks it's not fair that she is blamed for Maggie's mess.

• What should Linda do?

_____

_____

_____

_____

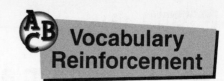

Choose the Correct Term

A. In each of the following sentences, the italicized word makes the sentence incorrect. Look at the terms in the box below to find the term that makes the sentence more correct. Write the correct term on the line. Use each term only once.

> **values**   **peer pressure**   **traditions**
>
> **cooperate**   **communicate**

1. My brother and I always *argue*, and that's why we work together and get along so well.   _____

2. Of all the *songs* my mother taught me, she said honesty and fairness were the most important.   _____

3. One of my favorite family *chores* is going to Grandma's house for Thanksgiving dinner.   _____

4. When I obey my parents' rules, it helps me resist *parties* from my school friends.   _____

5. I know that I can always talk to my mother about my problems because she and I *disagree* so well.   _____

B. Choose two vocabulary terms from the following list: *nuclear family, single-parent family, blended family, extended family.* Then, on a separate sheet of paper, write a correct sentence using each term.

Name _____

Living in a Healthful Community

Directions
- Use lesson vocabulary and other words in the Word Bank to complete each **Summary**.
- Read the section directions to complete each **Lesson Details**.

Word Bank

air	environment	natural resources	pollution	land
clean	solid waste	nonrenewable resources	safe	water
conservation	healthful	renewable resources	graffiti	EMTs

Lesson 1 pp. 304-307

Summary All the living and nonliving things that surround you make up your

_____. A _____ environment has clean

_____, _____, and _____.

Lesson Details Use pages 304–307 to give four examples of outdoor recreation.

_____

_____

Lesson 2 pp. 308-310

Summary Custodians and other workers help keep a community healthy by keeping

public areas _____ and free of trash and _____. Police

officers, firefighters, dispatchers, and _____ keep a community

_____ and help people in an emergency.

Lesson 3 pp. 312-315

Summary Materials from nature that people use to meet their needs are called

_____. Some resources, called _____, can
be replaced naturally. Resources that take a very long time to replace or cannot be

replaced at all are called _____.

Lesson Details Use pp. 312–315 to complete the sentences.

1. Three natural resources are _____ , _____ , and _____ .

2. Two resources that will never run out are _____ and

_____ .

3. One nonrenewable resource is _____ . It is considered nonrenewable

because _____ .

| Lesson 4 | pp. 316–321

Summary Sometimes natural resources contain harmful materials such as smoke,

chemicals, and _____ . These materials are _____ .

Lesson Details Use pp. 316–321 to complete the sentences about pollution.

People can help reduce air pollution by _____ , _____ ,

and using public _____ . Water pollution can be reduced if people

do not throw _____ into water. People can reduce land pollution

by _____ .

| Lesson 5 | pp. 324–326

Summary One way to keep the environment healthful is to conserve natural

resources. _____ is the careful use of resources.

Lesson Details Use pp. 324–326 to complete the graphic organizer about conservation.

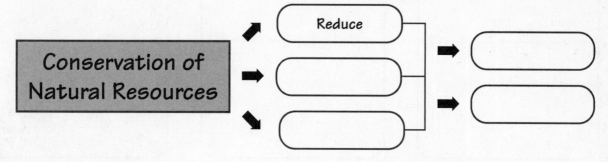

Conservation of
Natural Resources

Reduce

Draw Conclusions

The Story of Blue Lake

Today the town of Blue Lake received a trophy for doing the best job in the whole state of protecting natural resources. The mayor thanked all the people of Blue Lake for helping the town earn the trophy. The people of the town had set a goal of protecting natural resources. They worked together and met their goal. Blue Lake now has the most healthful environment in the state.

The people of Blue Lake knew they had reached their goal. Public buildings and parks were clean and free of litter and graffiti. Local factories had found ways to keep from polluting the air, land, and water with waste materials. The town bought land for a new landfill and recycled much of its garbage and other trash in the new recycling center.

After the award ceremony, a picnic was held in the town square. As you may have guessed, there were plenty of containers for trash and recycling.

Complete the graphic organizer to show why Blue Lake deserved a trophy.

What I Read:		What I Know:		Conclusion:
The people of Blue Lake succeeded in reaching their goal of protecting their natural resources.	**+**		**=**	

Life Skill

Set Goals

Steps for Setting Goals

1. Choose a goal.

2. List steps to meet the goal. Determine whether you will need any help.

3. Check your progress as you work toward the goal.

4. Reflect on and evaluate your progress toward the goal.

Use the steps to help these students set goals.

A. Matt and his friends like to play basketball on the neighborhood court. One of the backboards is cracked, the baskets don't have nets, and grass is growing through cracks in the asphalt. Matt decides he wants to get the basketball court repaired.

• How can Matt get the help he needs to repair the basketball court?

_____

_____

_____

_____

B. Kayla knows that she is careless about conserving energy. She usually forgets to turn off the lights or TV when she leaves the room. She often leaves her CD player on when she leaves for school.

• Use the Steps for Setting Goals to help Kayla make a plan for saving energy.

_____

_____

_____

_____

Name _____

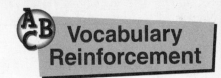

Word Puzzle

Read each numbered phrase. Find the term in the box that matches each phrase. Put one letter on each line.

> graffiti   conservation   renewable   natural resources
>
> pollution   solid waste   nonrenewable   environment

1. the careful use of natural resources

___ ___ ___ ___ ___ ___ ___ ___ ___ ___ ___ ___

2. writings or drawings put on a public building without permission

___ ___ ___ ___ ___ ___ ___ ___

3. all the living and nonliving things that surround you

___ ___ ___ ___ ___ ___ ___ ___ ___ ___ ___

4. able to be replaced

___ ___ ___ ___ ___ ___ ___ ___ ___

5. materials from nature that people use to meet their needs

___ ___ ___ ___ ___ ___ ___   ___ ___ ___ ___ ___ ___ ___ ___ ___

6. taking a long time to replace or unable to be replaced at all

___ ___ ___ ___ ___ ___ ___ ___ ___ ___ ___ ___

7. any harmful material in the air, water, or land

___ ___ ___ ___ ___ ___ ___ ___ ___

8. term for garbage and litter

___ ___ ___ ___ ___ ___ ___ ___ ___ ___